OOPS! ACCIDENTAL INVENTIONS

STICKY NOTES

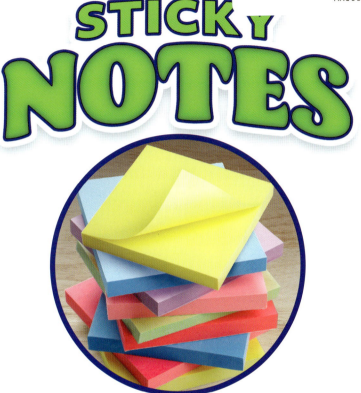

by Catherine C. Finan

Consultant: Beth Gambro
Reading Specialist, Yorkville, Illinois

Minneapolis, Minnesota

Teaching Tips

Before Reading

- Look at the cover of the book. Discuss the picture and the title.
- Ask readers to brainstorm a list of what they already know about sticky notes. What can they expect to see in this book?
- Go on a picture walk, looking through the pictures to discuss vocabulary and make predictions about the text.

During Reading

- Read for purpose. Encourage readers to think about sticky notes as they are reading.
- Ask readers to look for the details of the book. What happened to take the sticky note from an accident to a helpful tool?
- If readers encounter an unknown word, ask them to look at the sounds in the word. Then, ask them to look at the rest of the page. Are there any clues to help them understand?

After Reading

- Encourage readers to pick a buddy and reread the book together.
- Ask readers to name two things that happened when the sticky note was being developed. Find the pages that tell about these things.
- Ask readers to write or draw something they learned about the creation of sticky notes.

Credits:
Cover and title page, © Photoevent/iStock and © chalrumpon onnongwa/Shutterstock; 3, © archives/iStock; 5, © PeopleImages/iStock; 7, © CraigRJD/iStock; 9, © simonkr/iStock; 11, © Khosrork/iStock; 13, © Signe Dons/Wikimedia Creative Commons license 3.0; 14–15, © Ugur Karakoc/iStock; 16–17, © VAVSTYLE/Shutterstock; 19, © MR.Yanukit/Shutterstock; 20–21, © Zinkevych/iStock; 22TL, © subjug/iStock; 22MR, © Dmytro Skrypnykov/iStock; 22BL, © energyy/iStock; 23TL, © PeopleImages/iStock; 23TM, © elena_hramowa/iStock; 23TR, © Weekend Images Inc./iStock; 23BL, © Halfpoint/iStock; and 23BR, © Yobro10/iStock.

Library of Congress Cataloging-in-Publication Data

Names: Finan, Catherine C., 1972- author.
Title: Sticky notes / by Catherine C. Finan.
Description: Minneapolis, Minnesota : Bearport Publishing, [2023] | Series:
Oops! Accidental inventions | Includes bibliographical references and
index.
Identifiers: LCCN 2022034215 (print) | LCCN 2022034216 (ebook) | ISBN
9798885093460 (library binding) | ISBN 9798885094689 (paperback) | ISBN
9798885095839 (ebook)
Subjects: LCSH: Sticky notes--Juvenile literature. | Paperwork (Office
practice)--Management--Juvenile literature.
Classification: LCC HF5547.15 .F66 2023 (print) | LCC HF5547.15 (ebook) |
DDC 651.7/4--dc23/eng/20220908
LC record available at https://lccn.loc.gov/2022034215
LC ebook record available at https://lccn.loc.gov/2022034216

Copyright © 2023 Bearport Publishing Company. All rights reserved. No part of this publication may be reproduced in whole or in part, stored in any retrieval system, or transmitted in any form or by any means, electronic, mechanical, photocopying, recording, or otherwise, without written permission from the publisher.

For more information, write to Bearport Publishing, 5357 Penn Avenue South, Minneapolis, MN 55419.

Contents

A Sticky Accident 4

Sticky Notes Today 22

Glossary 23

Index 24

Read More 24

Learn More Online 24

About the Author 24

A Sticky Accident

Sticky notes help us remember things.

We can put them anywhere!

How did this helpful **invention** happen?

Say invention like in-VEN-chuhn

The **glue** on sticky notes was first made in 1968.

It happened by **accident**.

Oops!

Say accident like
AK-si-duhnt

Spencer Silver made this new kind of glue.

He wanted it to be very strong.

But it was **weak**.

Uh-oh!

The glue stuck to many things.

But it came off easily.

Spencer did not know what to do with it!

Spencer talked to a man named Art Fry.

Art had a problem.

His **bookmarks** kept falling out of his books.

Could Spencer's glue help?

Art used the glue to make a sticky bookmark.

It worked!

The bookmark stayed in place.

But Art could move it, too.

Then, Art and Spencer tried something else.

They put the glue on pieces of yellow paper.

These were the first sticky notes.

A few stores started selling the notes in 1977.

Not many people wanted them at first.

But soon, sticky notes became very popular!

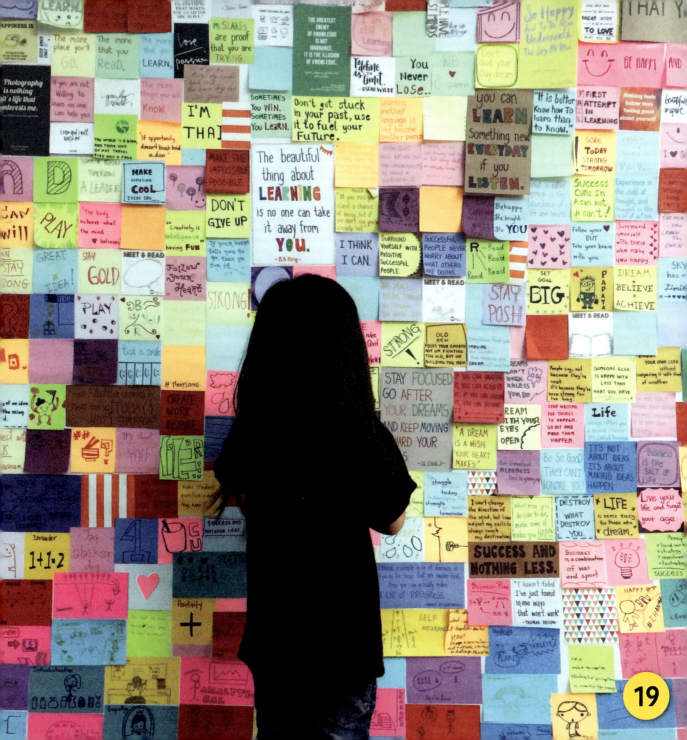

Today, sticky notes are everywhere.

People use them at home and in offices.

Kids can use them at school.

This is all thanks to a sticky mistake!

Sticky Notes Today

The longest line of sticky notes ever made was 114,741 notes long.

The first sticky notes were yellow. Now, they come in many colors.

The smallest sticky notes are the size of your finger. The biggest ones are larger than a school bus seat.

Glossary

accident something that is not planned

bookmarks strips of paper used to mark pages in books

glue a sticky liquid used to join things together

invention something new that people have made

weak not strong

Index

bookmarks 12, 14
Fry, Art 12–14, 16
glue 6, 8, 10, 12, 14, 16
paper 16
Silver, Spencer 8, 10, 12, 16
stores 18

Read More

Meister, Cari. *From Trees to Paper (Who Made My Stuff?).* Mankato, MN: Amicus, 2020.

Waxman, Laura Hamilton. *Cool Kid Inventions (Lightning Bolt Books: Kids in Charge!).* Minneapolis: Lerner Publications, 2020.

Learn More Online

1. Go to **www.factsurfer.com** or scan the QR code below.
2. Enter **"Sticky Notes"** into the search box.
3. Click on the cover of this book to see a list of websites.

About the Author

Catherine C. Finan is a writer living in northeast Pennsylvania. She uses sticky notes to help her remember just about everything!